PRAISE FOR
Things You May Find Hidden in My Ear

"Mosab Abu Toha's elegant and unforgettable poetry calls me to celebrate the struggle to survive. Though forged in the bleak landscape of Gaza, he conjures a radiance that echoes Milosz and Kabir. These poems are like flowers that grow out of bomb craters and Mosab Abu Toha is an astonishing talent to celebrate."

—MARY KARR

"Mosab Abu Toha is an astonishingly gifted young poet from Gaza, almost a seer with his eloquent lyrical vernacular, his visions of life, continuity, time, possibility, and beauty. His poems break my heart and awaken it, at the same time. I feel I have been waiting for his work all my life."

—NAOMI SHIHAB NYE

"Mosab Abu Toha's *Things You May Find Hidden in My Ear* arrives with such refreshing clarity and voice amidst a sea of immobilizing self-consciousness. It is no great feat to say a complicated thing in a complicated way, but here is a poet who says it plain: 'In Gaza, some of us cannot completely die.' Later, 'This is how we survived.' It's remarkable. This is poetry of the highest order."

—KAVEH AKBAR

THINGS YOU MAY FIND HIDDEN IN MY EAR

Cover and interior photographs by Mosab Abu Toha
Cover design by Gerilyn Attebery

ISBN: 978-0-87286-860-1
eISBN: 978-0-87286-888-5

Library of Congress Cataloging-in-Publication Data

Names: Abu Toha, Mosab, author.
Title: Things you may find hidden in my ear : poems from Gaza / Mosab Abu
Toha.
Description: San Francisco : City Lights Books, 2022.
Identifiers: LCCN 2021046542 | ISBN 9780872868601 (trade paperback) | ISBN
9780872868885 (epub)
Subjects: LCSH: Palestinian Arabs—Gaza Strip--Poetry. | Gaza—Poetry. |
LCGFT: Poetry.
Classification: LCC PR9570.P343 A28 2022 | DDC 821/.92—dc23/eng/20220113
LC record available at https://lccn.loc.gov/2021046542

City Lights Books are published at the City Lights Bookstore
261 Columbus Avenue, San Francisco, CA 94133
www.citylights.com

THINGS
YOU MAY FIND
HIDDEN
IN MY EAR

Poems from Gaza

MOSAB ABU TOHA

CITY LIGHTS BOOKS

Knotting poems from shards of glass, concrete, steel bars, isn't easy.
Sometimes my hands bleed. My gloves get burnt every time.

CONTENTS

THINGS YOU MAY FIND HIDDEN IN MY EAR

PALESTINE A–Z

A

An apple that fell from the table on a dark evening when man-made lightning flashed through the kitchen, the streets, and the sky, rattling the cupboards and breaking the dishes.

"Am" is the linking verb that follows "I" in the present tense when I am no longer present, when I'm shattered.

B

A book that doesn't mention my language or my country, and has maps of every place except for my birthplace, as if I were an illegitimate child on Mother Earth.

Borders are those invented lines drawn with ash on maps and sewn into the ground by bullets.

C

Gaza is a city where tourists gather to take photos next to destroyed buildings or graveyards.

A country that exists only in my mind. Its flag has no room to fly freely, but there is space on the coffins of my countrymen.

D

Dar means house. My grandparents left their house behind in 1948 near Yaffa beach. A tree my father told me about stood in the front yard.

Dreams of children and their parents, of listening to songs, or watching plays at Al-Mishal Cultural Center. Israel destroyed it in August 2018. I hate August. But plays are still performed in Gaza. Gaza is the stage.

E

An email account that I used when the power was on, the email through which I smelled overseas air. I used it first to send photos to my aunt in Jordan, who we last saw in 2000.

How easy it becomes to recognize what kind of aircraft it is: an F-16, helicopter, or a drone? What kind of a bullet it was: from a gunboat, an M-16, a tank, or an Apache? It's all about the sound.

F

Friends from school, from the neighborhood, from childhood. The books in my living room in Gaza, the poems in my notebooks, still lonely. The three friends I lost to the 2014 onslaught: Ezzat, Ammar, and Ismael. Ezzat was born in Algeria, Ammar in Jordan, Ismael on a farm. We buried them all under the cold ground.

Fish in our sea that the fishermen cannot catch because the Israeli gunboats care about sea life in the Mediterranean. They once fished at the Gaza beach with a barrage of shells, and Huda Ghalia lost her father, stepmother, and five siblings in June 2006. I walked in their funeral procession to the cemetery. Blood was still fresh on their clothes. They had poured out some perfume to cover the stench. Over time my hate for perfume grew intense.

G

How are you, Mosab? I'm good. I hate this word. It has no meaning to me. Your English is good, Mosab! Thanks.

When I was asked to fill out a form for my U.S. J-1 visa application, my country, Palestine, was not on the list. But lucky for me, my gender was.

H

If a helicopter stops in the sky over Gaza, we know it's going to shoot a rocket. It doesn't see if a target is close to children playing marbles or soccer in the street.

My friend Elise told me hey is a slang word and shouldn't be used. "English teachers would faint at what goes on today in written English," she said.

I

Images on the walls of buildings, a child who was shot by an Israeli sniper, or killed during an air raid en route to school. Her picture was placed on her desk at school. Her picture stares at the blackboard, while the air sits in her chair.

I wake up ill when gloomy ideas about what might've happened to me come in my dreams, what if I had stopped for a few seconds at the window when a bullet from nowhere ripped through the glass.

J

Once I sent a picture of my desk in Gaza to a friend in the United States. I wanted to show that I was fine. On the desk were some books, my laptop, and a glass of strawberry juice.

When I sent that photo, I was jobless. About 47% of people in Gaza have no work. But while writing these lines, I'm trying to start a literary magazine. I still don't know what to name it.

K

My grandfather kept the key to his house in Yaffa in 1948. He thought they would return in a few days. His name was Hasan. The house was destroyed. Others built a new one in its place. Hasan died in Gaza in 1986. The key has rusted but still exists somewhere, longing for the old wooden door.

In Gaza you don't know what you're guilty of. It feels like living in a Kafka novel.

L

I speak Arabic and English, but I don't know in what language my fate is written. I'm not sure if that would change anything.

Light is the opposite of heavy or dark. In Gaza, when the electricity is cut off, we turn on the lights, even in broad daylight. That way, we know when the power's back.

M

Marhaba means hi or welcome. We say Marhaba to everyone we see. It's like a warm hug. We don't use it, however, when soldiers or their bullets or bombs visit us. Such guests not only leave their shit, but also take everything we have.

My dad used to prepare milk for us with some qirshalah before school. I was in 3rd grade, and my mother was at hospital taking care of my brother. My brother died in 2016.

N

In 2014, about 2,139 people were killed, 579 of them were children, around 11,100 were wounded, around 13,000 buildings were destroyed. I lost 3 friends. But it's not about numbers. Even years, they are not numbers.

A nail is used to join two pieces of wood or to hang things on the wall. In 2009, the Israelis targeted an ambulance with a nail bomb near my house. Some were killed. I saw many nails on our neighbor's newly painted wall.

O

Yaffa is known around the world for its oranges. My grandmother, Khadra, tried to take some oranges with her in 1948, but the shelling was heavy. The oranges fell on the ground, the earth drank their juice. It was sweet, I'm sure.

In Gaza, we had a clay oven that our neighbor Muneer built for us. When my mother wanted to bake, I fed it wood stems or cardboard to heat it for the bread. The woody stems were made from dried plants: pepper, eggplant, and cornstalks.

P

A poem is not just words placed on a line. It's a cloth. Mahmoud Darwish wanted to build his home, his exile, from all the words in the world. I weave my poems with my veins. I want to build a poem like a solid home, but hopefully not with my bones.

On July 23, 2014, a friend called and said, "Ezzat was killed." I asked which Ezzat. "Ezzat, your friend." My phone slipped from my hand, and I began to run, not knowing where.

What's your name? Mosab. Where are you from? Palestine. What's your mother tongue? Arabic, but she's sick. What's the color of your skin? There is not enough light to help me see.

Q

We were watching a soccer match. Comments and shouts filled the room. The power was cut off, and everything became quiet. We could hear our breathing in the dark.

Al-Quds is Arabic for Jerusalem. I have never been to al-Quds. It's around 60 miles from Gaza. People who live 5,000 miles away can move there, while I cannot even visit.

R

I was born in November. My mother told me she was walking on the beach with my father. It turned stormy and began to rain. My mother felt pain, and an hour later, she gave birth to me. I love the rain and the sea, the last two things I heard before I came into this horrible world.

S

I like to go to the beach and watch the sun as it sinks into the sea. She's going to shine on nicer places, I think to myself.

My son's name is Yazzan. He was born in 2015, or a year after the 2014 war. This is how we date things. Once he saw a swarm of clouds. He shouted, "Dad, some bombs. Watch out!" He thought the clouds were bomb smoke. Even nature confuses us.

T

In summer, I drink tea with mint. In winter, I add dried sage. Anyone who visits, even if it's a neighbor knocking at the door to ask about what day or date it is, I offer them tea. Offering tea is like saying Marhaba.

They once said Palestine will be free tomorrow. When is tomorrow? What is freedom? How long does it last?

U

It wasn't raining that day, but I took my umbrella anyway. When an F-16 flew over the town, I opened my umbrella to hide. Kids thought I was a clown.

In August 2014, Israel bombed my university's administration building. The English department was turned into a ruin. My graduation ceremony got postponed. Families of the dead attended, to receive not a degree, but a portrait of their child.

V

When we moved from Cambridge to Syracuse, I looked out the window of the U-Haul van. What a huge country America is, I thought. Why did Zionists occupy Palestine and still build settlements and kill us in Gaza and the West Bank? Why don't they live here in America? Why can't we come here to live and work? My friend heard me. He was from Ireland. We both loved the Liverpool football club.

In Gaza, you can find a man planting a rose in the hollow space of an unexploded tank shell, using it as a vase.

W

One day, we were sleeping in our house. A bomb fell on a nearby farm at 6 a.m., like an alarm clock waking us up early for school.

In August 2014 after the 51 days of Israeli onslaught, the walls in my room had more windows than when I left, windows that would no longer close. Winter was harsh on us.

X

When I was wounded in January 2009, I was 16. I was taken to hospital and x-rayed for the first time. There were two pieces of shrapnel in my body. One in my neck, another in my forehead. Seven months later, I had my first surgery to remove them. I was still a child.

For Christmas, a friend gave the kids a xylophone. It had one wooden row. The bars were of different lengths and colors, red, yellow, green, blue, purple, and white. The kids showed it to their grandparents back in Gaza, whose eyes danced while the kids smiled.

Y

Yaffa is my daughter's name. I put my ears near her mouth when she speaks, and I hear Yaffa's sea, waves lapping against the shore. I look in her eyes, and I see my grandparents' footsteps still imprinted on the sand.

How did you leave Gaza? Do you plan to return? You should stay in the U.S. You mustn't think of going back to Gaza. Things people say to me.

Z

When I was in the fifth grade, our science teacher wanted us to visit a zoo, to see the animals, listen to their sounds, watch how they walk and sleep. When I went there, they were bored, gave me their back. They lived in cages in a caged place.

We use a zero article with most proper nouns. My name and that of my country have an extra zero in front, like when you call overseas. But we have been pulled down beneath the seas, do you see what I mean?

LEAVING CHILDHOOD BEHIND

When I left, I left my childhood in the drawer
and on the kitchen table. I left my toy horse
in its plastic bag.
I left without looking at the clock.
I forget whether it was noon or evening.

Our horse spent the night alone,
no water, no grains for dinner.
It must have thought we'd left to cook a meal
for late guests or to make a cake
for my sister's tenth birthday.

I walked with my sister, down our road with no end.
We sang a birthday song.
The warplanes echoed across the heavens.

My tired parents walked behind,
my father clutching to his chest
the keys to our house and to the stable.

We arrived at a rescue station.
News of the airstrikes roared on the radio.
I hated death, but I hated life, too,
when we had to walk to our drawn-out death,
reciting our never-ending ode.

WHAT IS HOME?

What is home:

it is the shade of trees on my way to school before they were
uprooted.

It is my grandparents' black-and-white wedding photo before the
walls crumbled.

It is my uncle's prayer rug, where dozens of ants slept on wintry
nights, before it was looted and put in a museum.

It is the oven my mother used to bake bread and roast chicken
before a bomb reduced our house to ashes.

It is the café where I watched football matches and played—

My child stops me: Can a four-letter word hold all of these?

MY GRANDFATHER WAS A TERRORIST

My grandfather was a terrorist—
He tended to his field,
watered the roses in the courtyard,
smoked cigarettes with grandmother
on the yellow beach, lying there
like a prayer rug.

My grandfather was a terrorist—
He picked oranges and lemons,
went fishing with brothers until noon,
sang a comforting song en route
to the farrier's with his piebald horse.

My grandfather was a terrorist—
He made a cup of tea with milk,
sat on his verdant land, as soft as silk,

My grandfather was a terrorist—
He departed his house, leaving it for the coming guests,
left some water on the table, his best,
lest the guests die of thirst after their conquest.

My grandfather was a terrorist—
He walked to the closest safe town,
empty as the sullen sky,

vacant as a deserted tent,
dark as a starless night.

My grandfather was a terrorist—
My grandfather was a man,
a breadwinner for ten,
whose luxury was to have a tent,
with a blue UN flag set on the rusting pole,
on the beach next to a cemetery.

ON A STARLESS NIGHT

On a starless night,
I toss and turn.
The earth shakes, and
I fall out of bed.
I look out my window. The house
next door no longer
stands. It's lying like an old carpet
on the floor of the earth,
trampled by missiles, fat slippers
flying off legless feet.
I never knew my neighbors still had that small TV,
that the old painting still hung on their walls,
that their cat had kittens.

PALESTINIAN PAINTER

Two birds
leave their nest,
singing a song, perhaps
for the artist working
in what used to be
a well-kept old garden.

He's painting a new house,
even a new garden.
Without shrapnel,
without twisted metal beams,
without broken bricks and loose electrical wires.

But then I see him hesitate,
looking at a headless doll
lying in the rubble.

I'm wondering if he'll paint it
as part of the new house and the resurrected garden.
It might destroy
its harmony.
It might disturb
visitors from abroad.

MY GRANDFATHER AND HOME

i

my grandfather used to count the days for return with his fingers
he then used stones to count
not enough
he used the clouds birds people

absence turned out to be too long
thirty-six years until he died
for us now it is over seventy years

my grandpa lost his memory
he forgot the numbers the people
he forgot home

ii

i wish i were with you grandpa
i would have taught myself to write you
poems volumes of them and paint our home for you
i would have sewn you from soil
a garment decorated with plants
and trees you had grown
i would have made you
perfume from the oranges
and soap from the skys tears of joy
couldnt think of something purer

iii

i go to the cemetery every day
i look for your grave but in vain
are they sure they buried you
or did you turn into a tree
or perhaps you flew off with a bird to the nowhere

iv

i place your photo in an earthenware pot
i water it every monday and thursday at sunset
i was told you used to fast those days
on ramadan i water it every day
for thirty days
or less or more

v

how big do you want our home to be
i can continue to write poems until you are satisfied
if you wish i can annex a neighboring planet or two

vi

for this home i shall not draw boundaries
no punctuation marks

PALESTINIAN STREETS

My city's streets are nameless.
If a Palestinian gets killed by a sniper or a drone,
we name the street after them.

Children learn their numbers best
when they can count how many homes or schools
were destroyed, how many mothers and fathers
were wounded or thrown into jail.

Grownups in Palestine only use their IDs
so as not to forget
who they are.

IN THE WAR: YOU AND HOUSES

You fight. You
die.
You'll never know who won or lost,
or if the war ever ended.

They didn't find a place to bury you.
They carried you on their shoulders,
wandered through the neighborhood,
stopped at your childhood school
and the old park.

The houses never saw you.
They've already packed their bags.
Dust has erected a tent in the corners.
Rust has landed with its worn-out clothes on the tap
and on the spoon.
It steals from the water its soft slide,
while you,
you sleep on moving sand.

SEARCHING FOR A NEW EXIT

The curtain,
heavy with fear,
does not rise.

As so often happens,
someone has turned off
the power.

We are powerless.

The oppressive air
tries to move in vain.

There is no light
to help me see
the boundaries of my state:

my nonexistent state.

I cannot find the words
in my Gazan Dictionary,
not even in my American Heritage Dictionary.
I cannot find any words
in my imagination
to fill in the gap.

Everything stolen by tornadoes
from the East and West
battering our theater again and again:

so many funerals.

The air
stirs suddenly,
making whistling sounds.
My spirits lift—no longer flagging,
searching for a new exit.

No applause.
The drama never ends.
The audience leaves
before I arrive.

FLYING POEM

Like a woman
hanging her laundry on the clothesline,
I hang my words
on the lines of my page.

Heavy, frightened words,
spread fear in my room.
They shrink
when exposed to the sun
of the reading eye.

My words
dry up.

The next day,
my brother, tired of
gazing at those fainting letters,
throws the book
in the drawer.

The sun sets behind
the eyelid.

The words in the drawer
swelter and stew in their sweat.

My little niece smells them.
She opens the drawer.
The words fly out.
The poem is free.
It lands in nests of migratory birds.
They sing it to the passing clouds.

SOBBING WITHOUT SOUND

I wish I could wake up and find the electricity on all day long.
I wish I could hear the birds sing again, no shooting and no
    buzzing drones.
I wish my desk would call me to hold my pen and write again,
 or at least plow through a novel, revisit a poem, or read a play.
All around me are nothing
but silent walls
and people sobbing
without sound.

DISCOVERIES

We are fine, even though we don't feel well.

Gaza is okay, although it has nothing to make her feel that way.

In Gaza, the sun shines and the moon flirts with the leaves of the
   orange trees;

However, Gaza's people come and go empty-handed:

No good news to give to their children,

no candy to sweeten their pale mouths,

and no light to read by.

HARD EXERCISE

In Gaza,
breathing is a task,
smiling is performing
plastic surgery
on one's own face,
and rising in the morning,
trying to survive
another day, is coming back
from the dead.

OLYMPIC HOPSCOTCH LEAP

We sit and drink tea
in the hot night of Ramadan.
Boys play hide-and-seek.
Girls hopscotch around.
Mothers chat and laugh.

A buzzing sound of drones flying
above my family and friends
stops the games, the chatting, and the laughter.

A missile fails,
only falling into farmland nearby.
Shrapnel cuts electric wires.
Dust tops off our tea,
like latte foam.

More missiles come flying in,
on the lookout for anything that moves.

Angels get hold of my infant niece.
We look around and find only
her milk bottle.

DEATH BEFORE BIRTH (DBB)

A pallid smile on the face of the sky.
A nightingale departs the wet earth
to start its day, looking for seeds to eat.
A drop of cold water falls from its beak
onto a lazy snail.

Everything is in motion:
the air, the branches on the trees.
An apple falls.

The sound of a drone
intrudes violently.
It fails to move on and
leave us alone for some seconds,
refuses to listen to music
or the whistling of birds.

People die.
Others are born.
For us,
the fear of dying before living
haunts us while we are still
in our mothers' wombs.

RUBBLE SALARY

Why doesn't the warplane heave some rubble
overboard after bombing
a house to increase the pilot's salary?
On the scale, stones and rebars are heavier
than souls.

COLD SWEAT

Drenched in sweat.
I can see the stars
through a bullet hole in the ceiling.
I run my hands through my hair.
My damp trousers
are sticking to my legs.

I hear a noise.
I look around.
There's no one else in the room.
I cannot feel my body.
I look in the mirror.
It was the chatter of my teeth.

TEARS

Tears trickle down my silent cheeks.
I feel embarrassed. I don't want to bother
them, nor any part of my body.

Everything around me wants to stand silent,
unmoved by the air or by my breath.
Everything wants to stop for this moment. Even our olive
tree bends when it sees the bomb fall. The tree's curly hair

touches the dry sand. Its many green eyes are
pierced by shattered glass,
the windows of our living room, kitchen, and bedrooms,
and my father's library, where a couple

of sparrows nest in a corner in the ceiling. The dust
from our destroyed house is still falling slowly onto
our neighbors' trees and rooftops. While the rubble
and metal bars, those are heavy, they

have already fallen quickly to pound the rough, scorched earth.
Now the sky sheds tears on us all, and the dust settles
onto the deformed stones, its makeshift grave,
until the wind blows it on to a safer space,

maybe into a van of VIPs crossing the border, out
and forever.

DESERTED BOAT, DREAMING

A deserted boat,
I sit alone
on the beach.

Waves approach,
trying to reach me,
as if to touch my hand,
tell me that I'm safe—
at least for now.

Seagulls fly overhead,
casting split-seconds
of shade and joy.

Darkness falls quickly
on a moonless night.

* * *

I find myself
drifting
on the sea.

A watery door
opens from beneath,
I am swirling, being whirlpooled

to a state
I've never experienced before.

I feel safe.
Safe for all eternity.

"Rest in peace,"
I hear my father say.
"You've found a better place."

THE WALL AND THE CLOCK

There is always that clock on the wall.
Every time I step into my room, I feel
curious, want to take it down, see
what's behind its face.
I want to see how old it has become.
My father bought it when I was a child.
I want to count its teeth
to know its age.

But the clock doesn't get old.
The numbers never change.
Only I do.

And then there's the rocking chair,
and I am sitting in it, just me
in the room, rocking back and forth,
doing nothing but
imagining the wall shouting to the clock,
"Stop ticking! You're hurting my ears."

I look at the cracks in the paint on the wall.
It's more than just the sound of the clock.
Shrapnel holes stare at me
whenever I enter the room.

(The clock wasn't harmed in that attack.)

I hurry to pull the batteries out of the clock.
I whisper to it:
I'll take you to the doctor,
even though it's not only you who's sick.

The paint stops peeling.

I take the clock to the clockmaker,
ask him to make it soundless.
He removes the clock's vocal cords,
patches its mouth shut.
I didn't see the teeth,
didn't ask the doctor.

At home, I put the batteries back.
The clock works silently.
It adds to the silence in the room.

I settle back into my chair, read some poems aloud
to break off the threads of silence that dangle
from the ceiling.

A cold night breeze seeps through the holes in the wall.
I tear out some pages I've finished reading,
stuff them into the small, shapeless non-closable windows.

I am two hours late for work the next day.

The clock wasn't set right after its "treatment."
Surely it would've alerted me
if it were capable of speech.

Number 4 falls from the clock's face
when I try to adjust the time.

As if a front tooth has fallen out.

Four days later,
my brother Hudayfah
passes away.

MY CITY AFTER WHAT HAPPENED
SOME TIME AGO

The noose is tightening around the city's neck.
Looters strip the city,
sell off its clothing and jewelry to the monsters in the sea.
Trees, bare and heads down, blow their yellow leaves,
trying to cover the private parts of houses:
bathtubs filled with warm water for the new
bride and groom.

In the stall, they are selling a photo of my young grandmother.
They don't know she began to smoke when she got older.
I wish I had a cigarette with me to put near the frame.
I once tried to light a cigarette and smoke.
I burned a finger and never tried again.

My grandfather's cane leans against a dusty wall
near my young father's school bag.

Two men hurriedly grab the books piled up below the table,
buy them for the first price the seller announces.
Their hands vomit them into the sea close by.
The words' eyes turn red with salt,
the maps drink too much, and
water floods their lakes and rivers, seeping out from the pages.

The city no longer exists except in the craters.
I have nowhere to go except down a new, untrodden road.

In Gaza, some of us cannot completely die.
Every time a bomb falls, every time shrapnel hits our graves,
every time the rubble piles up on our heads,
we are awakened from our temporary death.

Everything gets tied in Gaza's noose.

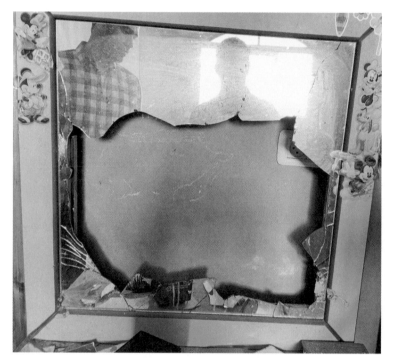

Where is the rest of me? Shattered in pieces.

When a shower of stones isn't enough, a sky of stones might be.

The scent of coffee still hangs in the air. But where is the kitchen?

I wanted to make tea for our guests, but a person from Porlock ruined the party.

Mid-Term Test

When a drone follows you on your way to school, what is it doing:

a. It's keeping an eye on you so you won't get hit by a car;

b. It's watching in case you lose your pocket money on the way;

c. It's counting your steps to make sure you're getting your daily exercise; or

d. It's covering your head in case an F-16 drops a bomb on you by mistake.

The seashells are filled with the sound of lapping waves,
our feet running on the sand,
and the stories we heard from our grandfather.
There is no space for the noise of a drone.

When someone scribbles something on it, the boat wishes it was a piece of paper,
ready to be placed into an envelope and mailed.
When a child fills a small bottle with sea water to take home, the boat feels jealous,
wishing it could fit into that bottle and leave the desert behind.

Through it all, the strawberries have never stopped growing.

WE LOVE WHAT WE HAVE

We love what we have, no matter how little,
because if we don't, everything will be gone. If we don't,
we will no longer exist, since there will be nothing here for us.
What's here is something that we are still
building. It's something we cannot yet see,
because we are part
of it.
Someday soon, this building will stand on its own, while we,
we will be the trees that protect it from the fierce
wind, the trees that will give shade
to children sleeping inside or playing on swings.

A LITANY FOR "ONE LAND"

After Audre Lorde

For those living on the other side,
we can see you, we can see the rain
when it pours on your (our) fields, on your (our) valleys,
and when it slides down the roofs of your "modern" houses
(built atop our homes).

Can you take off your sunglasses and look at us here,
see how the rain has flooded our streets,
how the children's umbrellas have been pierced
by a prickly downpour on their way to school?
The trees you see have been watered with our tears.
They bear no fruit.
The red roses take their color from our blood.
They smell of death.

The river that separates us from you is just
a mirage you created when you expelled us.

IT IS ONE LAND!

For those who are standing on the other side
shooting at us, spitting on us,
how long can you stand there, fenced by hate?
Are you going to keep your black glasses on until
you're unable to put them down?

Soon, we won't be here for you to watch.
It won't matter if you blink your eyes or not,
if you can stand or not.
You won't cross that river
to take more lands,
because you will vanish into your mirage.
You can't build a new colony on our graves.

And when we die,
our bones will continue to grow,
to reach and intertwine with the roots of the olive
and orange trees, to bathe in the sweet Yaffa sea.
One day, we will be born again when you're not there.
Because this land knows us. She is our mother.
When we die, we're just resting in her womb
until the darkness is cleared.

For those who are NOT here anymore,
We have been here forever.
We have been speaking but you
never cared to listen.

WE DESERVE A BETTER DEATH

We deserve a better death.
Our bodies are disfigured and twisted,
embroidered with bullets and shrapnel.
Our names are pronounced incorrectly
on the radio and TV.
Our photos, plastered onto the walls of our buildings,
fade and grow pale.
The inscriptions on our gravestones disappear,
covered in the feces of birds and reptiles.
No one waters the trees that give shade
to our graves.
The blazing sun has overwhelmed
our rotting bodies.

EVERYDAY MEALS DURING WARS

In previous wars, our neighbors would share meals with us in our
   basement. My brother would start a fire in the old brazier, and
   I would prepare tea and put the kettle on the burning coals.

There were truces every couple of days. My father could go out
   and check on the hens and ducks in their coops. My mother
   would climb the ladder to the roof to put water in bowls for the
   sparrows and pigeons.

Men would be taken to jails or concentration camps. They could
   see those who were fighting and killing them and their families.

Nowadays, we don't see those who take everything beautiful
   away from us. We don't even see our shadows during the day.
   The F-16s swallow the light from the sun, casting the shadows
   of their fat bellies on us, dead or alive.

Bombs punch the houses, knock them down, smash the
   fridges and the dishes. A house turns into a stew of
   concrete-and-blood.

We no longer share meals with the neighbors.

US AND THEM

I want to build my house on a swing.
I don't want to walk on this earth.

I tell them about houses being shelled,
about bodies
shred
into
tiny
pieces,
about a noisy sky and
ShAkInG ground.

And they,
they tell me about their concern over the little flowers
they haven't watered for hours,
over an ailing canary in the cage,
over a TV show they will miss tonight.

Their ears hurt when they hear sirens,
but we are made deaf by explosions.

Their muscles stiffen with fear on their way to the shelters,
while ours are pierced by boiling shrapnel.

SILENCE OF WATER

father typing on a keyboard
mother reading the morning paper aloud to
cover the sound of a neighbor's radio
hanging lamp swinging in the breeze from a cracked window
flies
losing balance
sometimes
b/w pictures on walls, searching for colors
kettle
on
stove
one big drop hammers the roof
no lightning, thunder, or clouds
it rains only on this house
dust and concrete
stuff the nostrils of other houses
water
on
stove
no longer boils
shrapnel has cut its throat.

ON GAZA SEASHORE

I convince myself that a palm tree never bends,
nor do its dates rot.
I imagine the sky only occupied by birds
and swollen clouds.
I walk alone along the beach and never fear getting drenched
by the cold, silent waves.

Should you find me asleep, be sure I am either
dreaming of roses and doves or staring into the void
beneath me.
I will dress in my rosy suit and walk to the port,
even though I know no ship is arriving.
My hope is that you will come flying to me
on your tireless wings.
I will collect seashells and pebbles to build a house
for us on the beach until you come.
I don't know how many houses I will have built
before you come.
I'm afraid I will rebuild Gaza by then.

SHRAPNEL LOOKING FOR LAUGHTER

The house has been bombed. Everyone dead:
The kids, the parents, the toys, the actors on TV,
characters in novels, personas in poetry collections,
the I, the he and the she. No pronouns left. Not even
for the kids when they learn parts of speech
next year. Shrapnel flies in the dark,
looks for the family's peals of
laughter hiding behind piles of disfigured
walls and bleeding picture frames. The radio
no longer speaks. Its batteries have burnt,
the antenna is broken.
Even the broadcaster felt the pain when the radio
was hit. Even we, hearing the bomb
as it fell, threw ourselves
to the ground,
each of us counting the others around them.
We were safe, but our hearts
still ache.

A VOICE FROM BENEATH

I want to drown myself in the silence of absence,
to fill my pockets with poems
and throw myself in a lazy river.

A distant voice calls upon me to build a room
from straw and clay,
to raise a black flag in the night,
to play the piano to the crossing owl.

A voice from beneath shakes my desk—
the ink spills on my drowsy pants.
It pummels my fingers and constricts my breath. It asks me
to stop writing heavy poems,
poems that have bombs and corpses,
destroyed houses and shrapnel-covered streets,
lest the words stumble and slip into the bloody potholes.

That voice takes away my voice.
It squeezes my poetry pages, tears them from
my head. Blood showers my curly hair.
My desk becomes crimson red.
Screams fill the cracks in the walls
and the potholes in the nameless roads.

SEVEN FINGERS

Whenever she meets new people, she sinks
her small hands into the pockets of her jeans,
moves them
as if she's counting
some coins. (She's just lost seven
fingers in the war.) Then she
moves away,
back hunched,
tiny as a dwarf.

GONE WITH THE GUNPOWDER

Even if the land is barren, it doesn't mean
no trees grew before.
If flowers do not blossom, the spring
never fails to come.
Our houses towered as high as our cypress trees.
We lit our streetlamps with olive oil.
Our houses no longer stand:

    Gone with the
gunpowder,

    the wind of
death, planted
beneath the warm soil.
The children's footsteps, the steam from
grandmother's teacup, the smoke from grandfather's
cigarette, flew into the black clouds, never looking
back.
The noise ahead pulled them by the neck.

    You can ask the sun.

    She saw everything.

    She wished she could stop,

stop the actors on the stage.

But her neck was tied to a rope.

And the villains,
they performed their role
even after the play was over.
And I, I have nothing.
I only write what I can hear
of the echo of that noise,
while my neck stretches from time to time
toward our distant houses,
hopeful I will be watching their seeds
when they sprout.

PALESTINIAN SONNET

After Wanda Coleman

Seized by echoes of suppressed words,
I surrender my memory as I flee for the maze.
I see signposts
directing me to retreat whenever I try to explore.
Every day I set foot in the maze, I close my ears
but the shouts of suffocated whispers
paralyze my shadow.

Letters slide from my mouth
into an icy river,
break the reflection of vapor
that emanates from melting clouds.

The chattering teeth of cold raindrops
drown out my throbbing silence.

It is not me who attempts to walk in the maze.
My withered umbilical cord tries to pull me
to my sick mother's bedside
before it is cut mid-nowhere.

IBRAHIM ABU LUGHOD
AND BROTHER IN YAFFA

The two walk toward the beach,
barefoot.

With his soft
index finger,
Ibrahim starts to draw
a map
of what
used to be
their home.

"No, Ibrahim, the kitchen
is a little farther to the north.
Oh, don't step over there,
Dad was sleeping there on the couch."

Tourist kids run by,
flying kites.
The waves hit
the beach,
shaded with cloud cover.

The mosque on the hilltop
calls for
prayer.

Ibrahim and his brother
still argue about where their kitchen was.
They both sit on the sand. Ibrahim
takes out a lighter, wishes he could make tea in their kitchen
for everyone on the beach.
Ibrahim looks upward to what used to be their kitchen window.
The mint no longer grows.

DESERT AND EXILE

for Men in the Sun

Which is vaster in the night, the desert or the dark?
Which is heavier on the sand, your feet or your fear?
Why don't you knock on the walls of the water tank?
Is sleep wrapping its thick rope around your mouths?

I can hear the sound of wheels on the moving
sand and the throbbing heart of silence.
The driver loses the map and takes you
to the earth where you will be
buried.
But all the prayers and anecdotes you shared
will be heard by the mirage of exile desert
and the bones of dead camels and horses,
whose riders are buried under the obliterated footpaths.

TO MAHMOUD DARWISH

His eyes are tightly closed, his glasses on the nightstand.
A pen and paper rest under his embroidered pillow,
waiting for the call of the muse.

He tells me how he once saw himself floating on a white cloud,
light glittering from above and beneath.
He didn't need his glasses to read the distant signboard under the
    moon.

I ask him why he has come for this long journey.
He says, "to return in a few hours."

He asks, "Do you know why I was born?"
"To live for some years and die."

He goes up Mount Carmel in Akka and returns to our table on
    the beach.

"I climbed the mountain only to return to the table."

He sips his bitter coffee and looks at himself in the mirror.
"I don't like to see myself on TV."
"That is pure narcissism," a friend whispers.
"Bastard, you are!" Mahmoud shouts.

"I am not afraid of death. I am ready but I am not waiting for it."

He hates waiting.

He asks death if it could wait for some time until he finishes
    writing his new poem.
He looks at himself in the mirror and puts
a fresh rose in his lapel for the coming long journey.

TO GHASSAN KANAFANI

Never thought that returning to Haifa
would lead to a bloody path.
Lakes were not full of water,
but mines.

When you opened the door to your car,
it wasn't the door to Said's house.
The old Polish Jew Miriam
didn't show up to let you into
your stolen home.
Death swallowed you and Lamees
down into its deep valley.

Shrapnel was the tattoo
marking your bodies
for the ghetto
of the Dead.

EDWARD SAID, NOAM CHOMSKY, AND THEODOR ADORNO IN GAZA

Dust tiptoes in a standing ovation
after the explosion.

Light hits the icy earth,
fades into the town's potholes.

Edward Said is out of place,
again:
His books fall from my shelves
onto the broken window glass.

> Palestine is also out of place:

Its map

falls off my wall.

Edward's exile bleeds again of wars,
of continued estrangement.

Chomsky, innately, repairs
the wounded words,
applying bandages
from his Universal Grammar kit.

Adorno tries to study the music

of the falling bomb
and shattering glass.

But the words slipping from the books
mystify his sight and mind:
the dust covers his glasses,
the musical score lies breathless
near his shivering feet.

DISPLACED

In memory of Edward Said

I am neither in nor out.
I am in between.
I am not part of anything.
I am a shadow of something.
At best,
I am a thing that
does not really
exist.
I am weightless,
a speck of time
in Gaza.
But I will remain
where I am.

TO IBRAHIM KILANI

Jerusalem didn't know you came not to visit it,
not to see and greet its mosques and churches,
not to smell thyme and sage in its narrow streets,
not to taste its freshly baked bread,
not to touch its olive trees,
but for it to see your soul leave
through tiny holes in its old walls.

THE WOUNDS

Israeli aggression against Gaza (December 27, 2008–January 18, 2009)

A Saturday, first day of the week in Gaza.
Age sixteen and after the first finals,
I finished my Arabic exam. I liked Arabic
as much as I liked English and soccer.
I discussed my answers with my father.
Home by noon, we stood on the roof of our house,
watched the pigeons my father raised as a hobby.

The limitless ceiling above us was part blue, part white.
Ships of clouds sailing slowly in windless sky.

A series of explosions shook the house, the neighborhood,
shook the earth,
words fell from my mouth, broke on my stiff, bare feet.

Birds from nowhere flew aimlessly in the open sky.
Some hid in trees.
The pigeons in their big coop trembled.

Rock pigeons, Egyptian pigeons, king pigeons,
and Halabi pigeons.

A tiny egg fell.

My answers must've fallen off the pages of my exam,
maybe melting from fear.

I saw black smoke rise from a building a few kilometers away,
blacker than the ink on my exam sheets.

We didn't hear the F-16s until they finished their strikes.
They descended from the inferno. Dante hadn't mentioned them.

About 80 F-16 aircraft with their bombs struck Gaza in unison,
like a big drumroll announcing someone's death.
But it was more than one death, I thought, it had to be.
We hurried to the radio, that old, dirty box
that usually vomits
blood and body parts into our ears,
hospitals full of burning wounds,
moans, a corpse, and a girl missing her leg,
lying on a cot
or a bloody floor.

Over 200 policemen killed and 700 wounded
in that dark hour. They had been training in police training
    facilities.
And two million other people
worried for their lives.

(Don't think of us as numbers.)

It was the first day of the year
when Israel targeted a neighborhood in Jabalia camp.
A Hamas leader named Nizar Rayyan was killed.
He was buried under the rubble of his house
with fifteen of his family,
mostly his children, the youngest aged 2.
On TV, I watched when a man pulled out a headless child,
another with no arm or leg. So small
I couldn't tell if boy or girl.
Hate ignores such details.

The houses were not Hamas.
The kids were not Hamas.
Their clothes and toys were not Hamas.
The neighborhood was not Hamas.
The air was not Hamas.
Our ears were not Hamas.
Our eyes were not Hamas.
The one who ordered the killing,
the one who pressed the button thought
only of Hamas.

My brother Hudayfah was born
deaf and mute.
He never grew up well either physically or mentally.
But emotionally, he was fine.
We didn't know that.

He was watching TV with us when videos and photos
of deformed bodies and limbless people appeared
on the TV screen.
Two days later, Hudayfah was hit,
inside, in a place we couldn't see.
We gave him a glass of water, he poured it on the floor.
He broke dishes, snatched the TV cord, bit his clothes.
We cried for him. We prayed for him.

Days later, he came back to us.

On the eighth morning of the Israeli attack,
the tanks rolled in and I heard bullets.
I peeked through our living room window.
(The living room was no longer living.)
I watched a tank on a hill near my school.
A bulldozer was building sand berms
for tanks and soldiers to hide behind.
We had no place to hide.
We dared not turn on the lights
or go up and feed the pigeons
or water the plants in our garden.

Our neighbors said we could stay with them.
They had a basement, more secure than our house.
We took some clothes and food and books
and the radio.

The Israelis fired shells randomly near our neighborhood.
Parents thought it wasn't safe to stay.

A few hours later,
we returned home quickly to stuff more clothes into plastic bags.
My dad said we would walk to our aunt's house in Sheikh
    Ridwan.
We prepared ourselves for the 40-minute walk.
It felt like ages of walking. We were dead and alive.

Death was hovering over us:

The Apache helicopters, the F-16s, and the buzzing drones.

We saw no one. Only lonely houses and motionless sand.
I saw some trees, green leaves beginning to pale.

200 meters away from our house,
I saw a yellow Mercedes stopped in the middle of a road,
nothing moving around it.
It had some cooking gas canisters and sacks of wheat flour
on its roof rack and in its trunk.
An Israeli bomb had killed the driver and others.
My friend's brother was one.
Mohammad Abu-El-Jidyan.
Age: 18.
A few other passers-by were wounded near the car.

The canisters had exploded, and the wheat
spattered on the ground.
Fresh bread baked with hot red blood,
and sand for yeast.

Next to it, a stalled ambulance,
the paramedic killed.
Arafah Abdel-Dayem
was my fourth grade science teacher.
I saw his blood and part of his scalp and hair
next to the wheels of the ambulance.
I was later told he'd been on his way to help those injured
in the attack on the yellow Mercedes.

The Israelis had used a nail bomb in the attack.
As a child, I never knew nails could kill people.
I thought they were only used in construction.
I was fooled.

My science teacher never taught us how a nail bomb works.
It wasn't part of his class.
My poor teacher, no one came to rescue him.

Dear teacher, did you know that after your burial,
the Israelis killed five of your family in the cemetery?
They didn't like how you were buried, it seems,
and hoped your family could improve with practice.

At that same ambulance attack, my new neighbor was murdered.
Ghassan Abul-Amrin,
barely 20.
(Now I'm older than he was then.)
Ghassan went out to buy bread for his mother.
He didn't return home. The family got worried,
turned on the radio to check if his name was announced.
This has been how we learn about our dead.

A hospital secretary who knew the family called that night.
He told them about an unidentifiable young man
lying the morgue, wondered if it was Ghassan.
News about Ghassan's death arrived,
not him.

My 3-year-old sister, Saja, was my companion on the journey out.
She grabbed my hand tightly.
My parents and siblings were walking behind.
We dared not look back to see them.
I had seven siblings at the time.

We dared not look behind and count them because
what if they became less?
Some bullets rained near our feet. The Israeli tanks
sat on a hill far away.
But for them, with their scopes and ammunition, we were very
    close.

Before we left, my dad had let the hens out of their house
to eat from our garden until we came back.

The pigeons were set free, too.
He was sure they'd return when we were back.

It's January in our aunt's house
when we fast on a holy day. My mother gives me 5 shekels
to buy some eggs and bread for my little sisters'
breakfast. I put on my small black slippers.
I put the coin in the front pocket of my hoodie.
I'm not happy. I don't like to fast.

Barely 16,
I'm on my way to the grocery shop
to buy some damn eggs.
I love boiled eggs.

I see a large crowd of people
gathering at the crossroad. I get curious,
I walk toward them.
Being small, I cannot see through the crowd.

A yellow light hits.
My head's split half open,
I feel this somehow.
The light might help me see more clearly, I tell myself.

Blood drips onto my eyelashes and hoodie.
In the brief moments standing there, I'm asking myself,
How come you can stand while your head is slashed open?

Everyone around me has collapsed to the ground,
fallen like beads of sweat.

I still stand. The picture freezes before me.

The smell of gunpowder crawls into my lungs.

Like a madman, I begin to run around.
Someone gives me a tissue to wipe the blood
on my left cheek and forehead.
I need much more than that.
It's not only my cheeks and forehead.
The shrapnel has also blown holes in my neck
and shoulder.

I'm no longer wearing my slippers, the 5 shekels
have disappeared.
I look around. People are rushing toward us.

A vehicle approaches. "Ambulance" it says.
But there is no paramedic, first aid, no bed to lie on.

Come on, it's my first time being wounded.

I get inside. Someone throws a corpse in next to me.
The body burnt, maybe no head. I don't look at it.
The smell is so bad. I'm so sorry, whoever you are.

The smell of death.

I open the window for fresh air.
The ambulance driver doesn't ask me how I am.

At Al-Shifa Hospital, people in and out.
I walk into the emergency room. No one looks at me.
I sit on the ground next to other wounded people.
Some lie on the floor like burnt matches.

A nurse who checks on me sees the hole in my neck
and the wounds on my face.
She starts to touch my abdomen and back to see
if there is any wound I cannot feel.

An elevator carries my gurney upstairs
to the radiology room.
A doctor tends to my wounds.
Someone is looking after me.

An hour passes. My father and brother walk in.

My brother points at the hole in my neck.
"Your index finger can fit in that hole.
It's centimeters from your windpipe."

If, when the rocket fell, I had moved my head a bit
to watch a bird on a tree or to count
the clouds coming from the west side,
the shrapnel might have cut through my throat.
I wouldn't be married to my wife,
father of three kids, one born in America.

My brother tells me:
Hearing the explosion and knowing you hadn't
returned home yet, we assumed you were dead.
We began searching for you in the morgue.

I look around me, relatives circle my bed.
I watch them as they chat. I imagine them praying round my
    coffin.

TO MY VISA INTERVIEWER

Which one of me do you plan to interview?
I am many, some I don't even know.
Need you interview my clothes, books,
toothpaste, comb?
My baby son's diapers and napkins?
The food not yet digested in my belly?
It will find its way out
before I get my visa.

It will have traveled before I do.

You will ask for my brothers' and sisters'
names.
Some have passed away. Will you need their names?
Do you plan to resurrect them?
I don't know all their birth dates.
I can only remember my younger brother's
death date.
He died on October 14, 2016.

You will ask for all physical addresses in
the past ten years.
We lived in north Gaza.
During every Israeli assault, we were displaced,
living in an UNRWA school, my aunt's house, or in the street.

You will ask for all email addresses and phone numbers
used in the past five years.
I used them only when the electricity was on
and when someone was there to respond.
I lost three dear friends in 2014: Ezzat and Ammar and Ismael.

You will ask for my web site.
I am no spider, and my site is wherever
a rose grows,
wherever clouds cast their shadows on
roofless houses,
wherever a bomb does not fall,
wherever a child does not confuse a cloud
for bomb smoke.

NOTEBOOKS

I walk carefully on the beach, look to
see if a child's footsteps lie ahead,
a child who's lost a leg, or two,
or can no longer hear the waves.

* * *

This angel of death just turned my body into pieces
and took my soul. It
left me lying there on the bloody ground,
my fingers resting on a neighbor's broken window.
It didn't look back to see if I was smiling or crying,
or if my mouth was even intact.
It just wanted my soul.
My family was out looking for my body.

* * *

During the night airstrikes, all of us turned
into stones.

* * *

When I hear the explosion, I can smell the sand, sand that blows
through the still air
to gather on my windowsill.

I can hear the little dog that barks whenever the branches of an
    almond tree stir.
He thinks it's a bird trying to scare him. Is it time to play?

The thick dust falling onto the tree and the dog, and blowing in
    through my window,
clears the confusion.

* * *

I turn off the lights at night so the F-16s
and their bombs don't catch me,
so the dust doesn't race in to cover my new clothes,
so the bullets don't hit my shoulders
when they cut through the skinless air.

* * *

I walked down the road and saw a tree.
I wrote a poem about its slim branches and vivid leaves,
a robin in its nest, watching a baby
in a stroller, a mother rolling up her sleeves.

The next day, I walked down and found the tree not there.
I hurried to my room, looked for the poem in my notebook.
The page was torn out.

I return to that road.
No tree.
I go back to my room.
The notebook is not there.

I look into the mirror,
and see a specter of my younger self.
I squat to pick up my pen from the floor.
The mirror follows me,
and shatters on my head.
I wake up.

* * *

Raindrops slip into the frying pan
through a hole in a tin roof.

* * *

We left the house,
took two blankets,
a pillow, and the echo
of the radio with us.

* * *

Why is it when I dream of Palestine,
that I see it in black and white?

* * *

People say silence is a sign of consent.
What if I'm not allowed to speak,
my tongue severed,
my mouth sewn shut?

* * *

Even the pens wanted to write about what they heard,
what shook them when they were napping
in the early afternoon.

* * *

The grave was brimming with sand
and prayers and stories that fell from visitors passing by.

* * *

It's been noisy for a long time
and I've been looking for a recording
of silence to play on my old headphones.

A BOY AND HIS TELESCOPE

A big white plane flies in the sky.
A child tries to see its passengers,
using his telescope.

A flock of migrating birds crosses by,
a stiff wind blows,
a mass of clouds pass,
the plane is gone.

Near the fence
the child needs no telescope
to watch the planes hovering in the air.
He can see the grenades,
the cameras.

A fierce wind roars.
The child hears
the buzzing sound of the drone.
Thick clouds cover the sky.
They blacken
after mixing with the smoke
of burning tires.

Threads of sun
hang in the air.
Butterflies flit across them

like the fingers
of a young guitarist
plucking the strings.

THINGS YOU MAY FIND
HIDDEN IN MY EAR

For Alicia M. Quesnel, MD

I

When you open my ear, touch it
gently.
My mother's voice lingers somewhere inside.
Her voice is the echo that helps me recover equilibrium
when I feel dizzy during my attentiveness.

You may encounter songs in Arabic,
poems in English I recite to myself,
or a song I chant to the chirping birds in our backyard.

When you stitch the cut, don't forget to put all these back in my
     ear.
Put them back in order, as you would do with the books on your
     shelf.

II

The drone's buzzing sound,
the roar of an F-16,
the screams of bombs falling on houses,
on fields, and on bodies,

of rockets flying away—
rid my tiny ear canal of them all.

Spray the perfume of your smiles on the incision.
Inject the song of life into my veins to wake me up.
Gently beat the drum so my mind may dance,
with yours,
my doctor, day and night.

MOSAB

My father gave me a difficult name.
Inside it sit two letters that don't exist in English.

My father didn't know I would
have English-speaking friends,
always asking how to pronounce my name,
or trying to avoid saying it.

But Dad, I like to hear others address me by name,
especially friends.

Even my name's root means difficult.
A camel that is described as Mosab
is one that's difficult to mount and ride.

But I'm not difficult in any way.
I will undress myself and show you
my shoulders, how dust has come to rest on them,
my chest, how tears have wet its thin skin,
my back, how sweat has made it pale,
my belly, how hair has covered my navel,
the spot where my mother fed me before birth.

The same spot, they say, the angel of death
will pierce to take away my soul.

And now, at night, my son's head hurts
when he rests it on my belly.

And my clothes, I feel them loose,
while others see them tight on me.

When someone from the life insurance company calls
and pronounces my name in English,
I see the angel of death in the mirror,
with eyes that watch me
crumbling onto this foreign ground.

MEMORIZE YOUR DREAM

Close your eyes
and
walk on the ocean.

Dabble your hands
in the water
and
catch the words
of your poem.

Write the words upon
the clouds.
Don't worry, they will find
their land.

Open your eyes.
In the night,
the sea is no longer blue.

Look around, and from
the falling
raindrops
choose your punctuation marks.

Put on your swimsuit,
dive deep down

and search for a title
for your epic.

Embark on your
moving homeland—
your boat.

Go to your bed
and, in your sleep,
begin to memorize
your dream.

FOREVER HOMELESS

Before my long travel, I pack
my suitcases, stuff them with
some sand from our land,
some scent from my mother's kitchen and
sounds of birds in the morning.

And in my pockets, I put the four
directions. My hands are the compass.

At the airport, I beg the officer
not to open the suitcases
and, if needed, to touch my clothes
gently.
Otherwise, I would be standing on nothing,
surrounded by nothing,
see nothing,
I would be weightless
and forever homeless.

A ROSE SHOULDERS UP

Don't ever be surprised
to see a rose shoulder up
among the ruins of the house:
This is how we survived.

MOSAB ABU TOHA
Interviewed by AMMIEL ALCALAY

Where were you born and where did you grow up?

I was born in a refugee camp called al-Shati Camp, which means Beach Camp, to the west of Gaza City. My father was born in the same camp, and my mother was born in Jabalia, the largest refugee camp in Gaza, and in the world. We lived in al-Shati, the third largest of the Gaza Strip's camps, until I was nine.

Then, in 2000, at the beginning of the Second Intifada, we moved to the town of Beit Lahia, which is a border town. From my window, I can see what used to be the settlements before Israel dismantled them in 2005. From our house I can also see the Israeli city of Ashkelon, which used to be called Askalan, al-Majdal, before Israel occupied it in 1948.

Where are you, age-wise, in your own family?

I'm the third. I should have been fourth but my eldest brother, whose name should have been Muhammad, died when he was very small. There was also a girl who was sick, but she died. And then my brother Hudayfa, who died a few years ago. We should have been ten, but we are seven.

And your grandparents, were they close by when you were growing up?

In my poems, when I talk about my grandfather, it is always the one on my father's side, I talk about something I lost, even before I could know it. My paternal grandfather passed away in 1986, a year before my father got married. So I never had the chance to see him. When they were forced to leave their home in Jaffa in 1948, my grandfather and his siblings, along with their aging father, moved south on trucks along the sea road, and settled in al-Shati. And they stayed, so whoever remains of that part of the family still lives in al-Shati. I never had the chance meet my grandfather, whose name was Hasan, and I don't know where his grave is.

And then there was my grandmother on my father's side, whose name was Khadra. Khadra died when I was eight. I only remember her smoking, sitting at the old doorstep to her small house, and whenever we children came, she would shoo us off: "Go away, go away!"

I didn't grow up in my grandparents' house. My father, upon his marriage, had to find a place to live with his young wife. Our situation was unlike many people my age who still were raised in a home with many generations.

And on your mother's side, were they also from Jaffa?

Yes, my maternal grandfather is still alive. My grandmother passed away while giving birth to one of my uncles. She was very young. My mother, when she was still a girl—and even after she got married—used to take care of her younger siblings, so she's like a mother to them. My grandfather still lives in Jabalia. When I think of a typical refugee camp, I remember my grandfather's house and the narrow streets, where you can only walk by yourself, single-file, two people can't walk next to each other.

How were memories of your family's roots in Jaffa transmitted to you?

Even though my father was born in al-Shati in 1962, he was the one to transmit those memories to me. I would always ask him: Daddy, can you tell me about my grandfather, Hasan? I would plead: Can you just tell me how his eyes looked? His hair? What he used to wear? What kind of work he did? I have only two photographs of him, and he is a kind of mystery for me. And I realize that this is like the rest of Palestine outside of Gaza: something I can hear about but not see or touch in person.

In 1967, three of my grandfather's siblings moved to different Arab countries, one to Egypt, one to Jordan, and one to Saudi Arabia. My grandfather stayed in al-Shati, along with his father and another sibling, and the three of them were buried here in Gaza. The three who left were unable to return because, like so many others, they didn't have Palestinian proof of identity.

Though we all have very different stories, as Palestinians our stories are the same in many ways. I think it's like we are living in a grave: we are not dead, we are going about our daily business, but in a grave. We are living in place of a dead person. I know that's contradictory.

During the last major Israeli attack in May 2021, we talked about your young daughter: she was very frightened by the bombs, but never asked who was bombing. In other words, for her, the bombing was simple reality. Can you somehow describe, as you were growing up, how you came to an understanding of what the situation of you and your family was?

In the first place, I never realized I was born in a refugee camp because that was just my world. I mean, a fish doesn't ask: Why don't we walk on the street and go shopping? A fish doesn't ask its mother why a shark is running after them. What does it want? Why does it want to eat us? A fish doesn't ask, Okay, mother, why is it not us who go after the shark? I mean, these existential questions are not asked, and I don't know why. I'm not even sure how we do come to comprehend these huge issues. I was born in 1992, and I think the first time I realized we were in somewhat of a dangerous situation was in 2000, when the Israelis struck a high-rise building in the al-Nassar neighborhood. I was in the street buying food for dinner. And I just watched an Apache helicopter shoot a rocket into a building.

You were about eight years old?

Yes, and I was not aware of whether I should be afraid or not. I didn't know what that helicopter was doing. I mean, I didn't understand what was going on. And then I started to see crowds on TV, carrying a bier, chanting and expressing their anger. It was a march, and the first thing I saw, as I would learn, was Muhammad al-Dura being carried on the shoulders of thousands of people in the street. And I started to cry. I'm not sure why, but seeing a kid who is nearly your own age, unable to move, and all these people— why are they carrying him?

That was the tragic incident of the boy, Muhammad al-Dura, who was being shielded by his father when they were caught in a cross-fire on the second day of the Second Intifada in 2000. The boy was shot, falling at his father's side, and those images circled the globe.

I started to cry. I was, and I am still very sensitive when it comes to seeing people suffering or maimed, or seeing blood. I just burst into tears.

When we moved to Beit Lahia, we didn't have windows. We just covered the openings where those would eventually be with some plastic. And in 2004, when I was 12, that was the first time I could sense the movement of Israeli tanks, a few hundred meters from our house. We didn't know whether we should just keep quiet: What if they hear us? When you are in danger, you imagine yourself to be the only target on planet Earth. This is a very strange feeling and not all people can understand it because, you know, not everyone has lived through an armed struggle. Even during this latest attack, wherever you are during the violence, you think the Israelis are watching only you. If you're in the street, even in your home, you think they are watching you in particular. This is the fear, the threat of knowing you can be bombed at any time.

Where did you begin to find poetry?

Poetry has always been part of our curriculum in Palestine. I'm talking about Arabic poetry, the huge names, like 'Antarah Ibn-Shaddad, Imru al-Qays, Abu al-Atahiya, Abu Tamman, al-Mutanabbi, Abu Nuwas, and then moderns like Ahmed Shawqi, Nizar Qabanni, Samih al-Qassem, Mahmoud Darwish, of course. So we have always been reading these poets. Pretty much every-thing that we read was in classical form, but I never tried to master the classical structures of writing poetry. When I think of poetry I don't think of Arabic poetry or English poetry or Spanish poetry. No, I just think of poetry as an idea, not as rigid form that I need to follow. The word for poetry in Arabic, *sha'ir*, doesn't refer to a particular form, it only has to do with feeling. So you have to be an expert in showing your feelings on paper or reciting your poetry to people so that they can feel what you're feeling. It can be an image but it does have to leave an impact on the reader. And if you can make them cry or smile, then you are a poet; if you can make them shiver, then you are a poet.

When you are a poet, you need to be saying something that cannot be said by other people. Poets don't necessarily need to be first-rate readers of poetry, because when they start to write poems they already have what they need, they've been living it. When I tell my story—to anyone—it's as if I'm reciting poetry.

The story that we are living here is something like an epic. When I think of the events of my life so far, being born just a few months before the Oslo Accords in 1993, and then the establishment of the Palestinian Authority in 1994, the Second Intifada in 2000, the 2004 invasion of Gaza, the dismantling of settlements in 2005, Hamas winning the election in 2006, then the siege in 2007, the major attacks by Israel in 2008 and 2009. Then the seven-day attack on Gaza in 2012, then most aggressively in 2014 and, very recently, the May 2021 attack. It never stops. I don't think that poets necessarily need to be living in a poetic milieu.

When did you become interested in studying English?

We were taught English starting in the fifth grade. Now they start in the first grade. I vividly remember that I was the best student in my class, but only in English, not in Arabic or mathematics. When I finished high school, my father suggested that I should think about going to the Police Academy, he said maybe I could become an officer. So I registered for the Police Academy but I didn't know what to think about it: I would be in an office somewhere, and sent to solve a problem here or a problem there, but I don't like being involved in problems. I told my father: I think I need to enroll in the English department. I went to the Islamic University of Gaza and I was accepted, and it started from there.

English grammar was one of my favorite things to study, the structure, the rules for English syntax. And then there was literature, but I majored in English language teaching. I didn't major in English literature because there had to be a purpose, and I wanted to be a teacher, so I could start earning money, make a living, and build something for me and my family. And, of course, I wanted to help my parents who have been in debt forever.

As you advanced, what kinds of things were you attracted to reading, what are the things you most remember?

I started to like English literature when I took a class in Romanticism. I don't know why, it was the Romantic poets, with their fantastic poems, I mean, William Wordsworth's "I wandered lonely as a cloud," I cannot forget this opening line. It gave me another world to think about and live in. And Percy Shelley, and Samuel Taylor Coleridge with "Kubla Khan." This class gave me a lot of things to love. Then there was George Orwell and his *Animal Farm* and *1984*, *The Wasteland* by Eliot. Those magical things that happen in literature: for example, *Doctor Faustus* by Christopher Marlowe. I mean, someone sells his soul to the devil—oh my god, what are you talking about, you're talking about a world that I want to be involved in, a world that does not exist here. I want to escape into that imagined world.

But when we talk about literature in general, you are not only talking about fantastic worlds or imagined realities. No, you are talking about works that document the lives of those authors and the places they lived. When I'm reading Wordsworth or Marlowe I'm not reading their beautiful words and sentences—no, they are telling me what they see. It's not only about the work of literature, but what is carried in it. And when I talk about Wordsworth and Coleridge and Shelley and Keats, I'm not talking about things they liked or wanted to bring to us. When I read them, I want to be there with them because I'm deprived of that nature and those things that exist in their world. When they tell me about the trees, the rivers, the clouds, the flowers, they are inviting me to live their experience, which is a very good way for me to travel outside Gaza. So I'm traveling through their poems.

You live a very harsh reality. By traveling through the poems, what does that do to your spirit?

It is a fact that we live under siege, and we live under an unceasing war of attrition. But there are some beautiful things around me: there is the sea, there are the clouds, there are flowers and trees and lemons on the trees, and these are things to enjoy, even if it is a momentary thing. And when I read poems, sometimes I see things around me that I don't usually notice until I read about them in a poem. Oh, this lemon, it really looks like the lemon this poet in Europe talks about.

In other words, the poem is never an escape, it's a return to a reality that is actually there.

Exactly! It's truly a returning device for me to be able to see these things again. And I think it's also a beam that sheds light on things that I sometimes—I'm not talking about myself as a poet, but as a reader, as a person—see as normal, but these things are not normal. When I read and see things depicted in a poem that resemble what I see in my garden or in the street, I realize that we are living on the same planet as Wordsworth. The lemon in a poem, it might be the same lemon I saw on the tree; when he's talking about the sun, it's the same sun. I'm invited to notice and enjoy things that I usually can't see when I'm afraid. So, to me, as a reader and poet, poetry can show things I never saw before. It also can bring my attention to something I saw but never enjoyed. And lastly, it assures me that I live on the same earth that Shakespeare, Wordsworth, Coleridge, and others inhabited.

So you are brought back to some sense of common humanity.

Yes, as Mahmoud Darwish wrote: "We have on this earth what makes life worth living."

When did Darwish become second nature, where something happens and you think of a line by him?

Of course, Mahmoud Darwish was part of the curriculum. Who can forget his early, revolutionary poem "Write Down, I'm an Arab"? or his "To My Mother," which Marcel Khalife sang. But I admire Darwish because he never stopped discovering himself. When you read Darwish when he was 19 or 20, as the young defiant Palestinian, and then you read the Mahmoud Darwish who traveled and lived in Haifa, Moscow, Cairo, Beirut, Tunis, Paris, Jordan, and finally Ramallah, you see how much he changed, and how much his perspective widened. He's not only a Palestinian poet, but he is also a universal poet. When I started to read his existential poems, his spiritual poems, his elevated poetry, I started to find part of myself in this world.

You know the section in Memory For Forgetfulness *where he arrives to Beirut and asks the taxi driver to take him to Damour so he can see the place he had been a refugee as a child, leaving Palestine? And he asks: What was I looking for? Was I looking for Ithaca, was I looking for the lost homeland, or was I looking for the child I had once been?*

I think I drew the idea of my poem about leaving childhood behind from this passage by Darwish. When Mahmoud Darwish left the village of al-Birwe at the age of six, what he left wasn't the family house or his clothes. I think what he left behind was the person whom he could have become if they weren't forced to leave that place. So the child he was in Lebanon was not the same child he could have become in al-Birwe. And this speaks to me directly: there are many Mosabs in the world—the Mosab who was born in Gaza in al-Shati Camp; the Mosab I could have been if my grand-parents were not expelled from Jaffa. Maybe I wouldn't have had to write poetry, maybe I could have been a chemist like Primo Levi or a linguist like Noam Chomsky. I could have been a scientist or a historian or a researcher of marine life. But now I'm living in Gaza. And I don't feel that I was a child, I think I was running from something. Maybe from my childhood. Maybe my childhood was left behind forever, because I never felt that I was a child. My parents never took me on a journey, my parents never boarded a plane and took the family to visit our relatives in Jordan or in Saudi Arabia. And there is a very important point here: in school, in textbooks, especially in social studies and in geography class, there is always an activity on the margin of the page—students take a field trip with the teacher to a mountain or a river or to the Dead Sea and see the level of the salt and how we float. But none of this ever happened for us. So I never exercised my childhood. I think it's there waiting for me—till when? Maybe until I go back to Jaffa and become a child again.

There is that great short story by Ghassan Kanafani whose title says it all: "He Was A Child That Day." In other words, he was not a child on all the other days. You and your wife have three kids, how do you think about this?

When I became a father, I started to love my parents more. This doesn't mean that I ever underestimated them but I started to love them more because I could see how much I love my kids. I could understand how much my parents used to care for me. But because I was a child, I was never aware of it. And because, as I mentioned previously, I didn't exercise my childhood, I sometimes feel sad because I tell myself: maybe I can give my kids the things that I wish my parents had given me. But I just can't do it. I cannot protect them during Israeli attacks, I cannot just take them on a journey, I cannot leave Gaza whenever I want with them. I wonder if my children will have a better future for their own children.

In your poem "The Wound," you go into detail about when you were wounded, at the age of 16. How do you think about that now?

When I think of that specific poem, I wonder about those very little kids who were buried under the rubble of their houses. They were unable to grow up, like me, and master the language to talk about their experiences. I was very lucky because I am fluent in English and Arabic so I can express my feelings and my experiences, write them down and document the wounds in my body and my soul. Right now, just a few weeks ago, the Israelis launched a massive and destructive war against Gaza, many families were erased from the civil history of Gaza, the roll call of people who live in Gaza. It's not easy to think about it—as I watch my kids at the ages of six and four and one, unable to take in everything going on around them—should I write on their behalf? But what I am writing is different from what they are living. I can express, for example, how my little daughter was trying to hide from the bombs and then her older brother gave her a thin blanket to hide under. I can describe this in a poem, but I can't express what it felt like to them to be hearing the bombs while not knowing that this isn't a game or someone trying to scare you and play with you, but this is about life and death.

What do you think happens to people who cannot find a way to process and express what has happened to them?

It means that what they have lived through will not leave them, so it will all come back to them in their nightmares. One function of poetry is to heal the wounds. These ideas in my mind, I don't really know what they are until I put them on paper. People who are unable to go through this process, of getting rid of things, transferring or transforming them, lose their mental well-being, their psychological balance. If they can't write, or deal with their nightmares by reading, by putting them on paper, or somehow sharing their feelings with other people, this deepens the wounds. These nightmares will continue to come up, in their dreams and their reality—it's very hard. One way of dealing with it is just telling it to other people and writing it down so you can know what disturbs you. I often think of writing about all these hideous ideas and these hideous events and just setting them on fire, so that I can burn these nightmares.

When there is a death or a demonstration and people are marching and chanting, it's very theatrical, a way of processing, and it also seems that people are highly aware of presenting a certain face to the world.

Yes, of course. Gazans have to show the world that they cannot be defeated. When a building housing a theater was destroyed in an attack in 2018, for example, many musicians came to play their music on the ruins of that building. When the Italian tower complex was hit by the Israelis in 2014, a young artist painted many different faces on the destroyed walls—gloomy faces, hopeful faces—looking toward the sky. It's very difficult that we have to do these things, but we cannot tell the world that we are giving up.

Tell me about the attack on your university in 2014, what you experienced then?

I was just a month away from official graduation. We had just finished our exams. The Israeli forces launched their attacks on

Gaza on July 7th and it went on for over six weeks. For statistics, official numbers say that 2,251 Palestinians were killed and 11, 231 were wounded, almost all civilians, of course, and many children and women. Ten percent, at least, of those people, have permanent disabilities. About 18,000 housing units were destroyed, leaving about 100,000 people homeless. Also 262 schools were targeted, seventy-three medical facilities, including hospitals, clinics, and ambulances. The power plant, sewage and water treatment facilities, of course. On the Israeli side, there were 71 casualties, 67 of them soldiers, and 469 soldiers and 261 Israeli civilians injured. There is plenty of documentation, but this is just to give some idea of the enormity of the imbalance, the asymmetry.

The Israelis bombed the administration building of my school, the Islamic University of Gaza. The English department was destroyed. The many books resting on the shelves of my professors were just lying under the rubble of the building. The first book that I could extract was the *Norton Anthology of American Literature*. Of course, it's very ironic that we in Gaza and Palestine read and appreciate and value American literature, and English literature, we study it, we just love it. And we try to imitate it, just as we imitate Arabic literature. But then all of a sudden, a rocket, or a heavy bomb that was paid for and manufactured in America, is killing, not only me, but the books that we read and studied in classes. That was very ironic to me.

I lost two dear friends, Amar and Ezzat, may God have mercy on them. Amar studied Arabic literature and he had a beautiful voice, particularly when chanting the Qu'ran. Amar was very popular, while I've always been shy. But I also have a good voice and, once, when I was chanting the Qu'ran, he came to me and whispered:

"Mosab, how did you do that? Can you repeat that, can you show me how you did that?" I told him that I didn't know, it just came naturally to me. And so we became very good friends.

I first learned about my friend Ezzat's death when I was out with a foreign journalist from Spain. I was translating for her at Shifa, the biggest hospital in Gaza. A friend called and said that Ezzat was killed in an attack, so I asked: Who? Which Ezzat? He said, Your friend Ezzat. I asked the journalist if I could leave. I got a taxi to Beit Lahia, heading towards Kamal Adwan, the central hospital in North Gaza, and as we were arriving, I saw a crowd of people. As I got out of the taxi, I saw my younger brother, Ezzat's father, and some neighbors. They were carrying Ezzat's motionless body on their shoulders. I was just trying to get close, to be close to his body. And then we went to the mosque. We prayed the prayer for the dead, and then he was buried. That was how I saw him for the last time. We were schoolmates and we shared the love of soccer. Once we went to a sports shop and got jerseys of our favorite team, Barcelona: I got number 14 and he got number 10. We used to go to the cafés and watch all the important games. I remember him telling me that his biggest dream would be to go to Spain and play for Barcelona. When the war against us finally ended, I visited his family to offer my condolences. I asked Ezzat's father to take me to his room and I opened the closet door and saw his Barcelona shirt, number 10, and asked if I could have it. So now I have both shirts.

And how did the idea of the Edward Said Library come about?

I went to the University during a ceasefire with a friend and I saw that *Norton Anthology* under the rubble. I posted my photo

115

holding the rescued book on social media and next to it put another photo of our house, partially destroyed by an Israeli airstrike on our neighbor's house. There were three holes in the wall of the room that used to be our home library. Friends started offering to send me books to replace what I had lost in my own small library. I created a social media page: Library and Bookshop for Gaza, and more and more people started to send books until I had about 600 books in my house. Some media outlets came to do interviews with me, and word got around so I started a fundraising campaign.

How did Edward Said come into the picture?

I knew his ideas, I had read some essays, but I had never come across any of his books. Not in my undergraduate years. Unlike Mahmoud Darwish, whose poems are taught everywhere, Edward Said was not well known in Gaza. I don't want to generalize, but my impression is that a lot of Palestinians in Gaza and the Occupied Territories were not so aware of the importance of Edward Said. Perhaps it was because of his political viewpoints, his denouncement of the Oslo Accords, what he thought of Yasser Arafat as a person. Said was despised by a lot of people in the political systems in Palestine and the Arab world. Which means that ordinary people absolutely should know about Edward Said.

By naming the library after Said, I think I was honoring the library and not him, because he surely deserves more than this. But because of the library, many people started to search for Edward Said, and many realized how much they had been missing.

Tell me more about the library, and how it developed.

I first started to collect books in my room. I then created a social media page to reach more people. When I had 600 books in my room, al-Jazeera English wrote a great essay about me and the library. American poet Katha Pollitt got in touch with me, and she was very helpful. I launched a fundraising campaign. I asked Katha if she could write about the library for *The Nation*, which she did. The campaign reached more and more people that way.

Of course, everything related to Gaza is a problem—I had to figure out how to transfer the money we raised, because it would be suspect if I wired it to my personal account. I couldn't get a license for the library because of the rift between the Palestinian Authority and the Hamas government in Gaza. The Authority in the West Bank issues the licenses, which would enable us to open a bank account for the library. However, there was no means to contact the government in the West Bank. This is typical. Therefore, I had to work with an existing Gaza youth organization. Eventually we found Middle East Children's Alliance, through Edward's widow, Mariam Said, and that has worked very well. Mariam was very excited and very supportive, as was their daughter Najla, and the whole family.

Can you talk about the kinds of activities that take place in the library?

It really functions more like a cultural center. The activities are not just centered on books and reading or writing. There are various youth initiatives, in music, in drama, in painting and drawing, et cetera. Literary groups come to meet. There are lectures and training sessions for parents and community members. Computer training. Workshops in how to protect against COVID, for example, and in psychological well-being. In some sessions, a trainer reads stories to kids to try and identify trauma so they can find some psychological or therapeutic treatment. It's much more than a library—there are two million people in Gaza, and there are not enough resources. I was born in a refugee camp, and I never saw a library in my life until I grew up and saw a small library run by UNRWA, the UN Refugee Agency.

We know there are huge problems in Gaza. And without going into statistics and deep analysis, I just want to get your reaction to a few major things. Tell me something about the meaning of water for you in Gaza.

We start with the undrinkable water that Gazans must drink every day, unpotable water. And the pools of water in the street after a rainy day, because there isn't a functioning drainage system, especially in the refugee camps. Water just invades the houses of people in the camps.

When I think of water, I remember the sea. The sea is one of the most beautiful things to look at. But, at the same time, it's linked to bloody memories. I have two in mind: in 2006, Israeli warships fired missiles at families on the beach at Beit Lahia, right where I live, and a whole family was killed. And the girl, the only survivor, was Huda Ghalia, she was I think 12 or 13. Instead of sitting with the family, eating watermelon, drinking tea, dancing, maybe mounting a horse, running around on the beach, the family turned out to be going—not on a trip or a journey—but to their death. And I remember this girl, blaming herself because she was the one who insisted that she and

118

her family go to the sea that day. So she blamed herself: 'I was the cause. I drove them to their death.' Another incident was in 2014, when four children from the Bakr family were killed playing soccer on the beach. I think the ball was the only survivor of that game.

I can also think about the water tanks on our rooftops that empty when the electricity is cut off. Then you don't have water for a few days and you wash your hands or your face by pouring water from a bottle, and the dishes by filling a corner of one container and rinsing in another. Primitive.

And then there is the sound of rain clattering against the tin sheets and siding in the refugee camps. It can be a good experience, the noise letting you know that it's raining, but for the people living in those houses, that noise just doesn't stop, no one can sleep, and if there are any little holes in the roof, then everyone has to move away from the dripping rain and bring out the buckets.

And the electricity, as you mention, is often cut off.

We are technically deprived of electrical usage. When the electricity comes back on, you can hear people shouting and screaming and clapping, as if someone scored a goal in the World Cup Final. People leave a ceiling fixture on so that when the electricity comes back, they will know. When you get four hours of electricity, and in winter, usually just two hours, what do you do with those two hours? Are you going to charge your phone or your laptop, if you have one, or wash the clothes? Are you going to watch TV, or are you going to look at yourself in the mirror at night? And what about the people who need it for their lives? Hospitals, dialysis equipment, cancer patients, ventilators. And then there are factories and shops. You always have to calculate how much food to buy, because you can lose a lot of it if the electricity schedule changes. You have to think about everything in this way.

The median age in Gaza is very young. Earlier you spoke of asking your father for stories about your grandfather, and how important that was for you. But there are fewer and fewer people who have memories of life outside of Gaza. I'm wondering if you can say something about this.

Unfortunately, it's not only about memories of our grandparents, but it's also their memories that are being lost, those are what we need to hear and memorize and then transmit to our children and grandchildren. But I'm also so saddened to think about my generation, our memories, being required or expected to tell our own stories of what happened to us in Gaza. I mean, for example, in 2021, 2014, 2009, or 2008. All the massacres and attacks on Gaza. Maybe our grandchildren will not ask us about Jaffa and Acre and Haifa. No, they will ask us about the 2014 war. What happened to you? What did you eat, which of your friends was wounded, did you leave your home, where did you go? This is a prolonged state of exile and estrangement and expulsion and ethnic cleansing. Our grandparents were driven from their homes and their cities, and any trace of them has been erased and replaced by something else, which is now called Israel. But we, their descendants, were also robbed of our right to dream and think about those places—no, instead, we are forced to live in the nightmares of our own current life. And they are creating more misery for us, wounding us again and again, so that we forget those earlier wounds in the face of the fresher wounds. The more the Israelis attack us, the more they are trying to erase the older memories. So it also becomes a matter of exhaustion.

Yes, the exhaustion of resilience: sumud, *the state of being steadfast.*

Why do we demonstrate our resilience? Is it because we think we should stay resilient or because we don't want other people to see us as weak? Or is it because we believe that what is happening to us is not going to last forever? And that what is happening to us is similar to what has happened to other people? I don't know. Sometimes I think I'm forever stuck in Gaza, even after having left it once, for the first time.

You were invited to be a Visiting Fellow in the Scholars at Risk Program at Harvard, but you arrived just a few months before the pandemic because of all the delays in leaving Gaza. I think we would need a whole other interview to go into the details of what it means to travel from, and then return to, Gaza. Suffice it to say that each trip took several months of waiting and preparation, often in different countries, at great expense and stress, with no assurance whatsoever of the certainty of actually getting 'permission.'

These are all forms of collective punishment that we are constantly subjected to, for the most basic rights: drinking water, ability to move freely, keeping families together, getting medical care, and so on.

Once you finally arrived in the U.S., what were your first impressions?

It was the first time in my life that I boarded a plane, at the age of 26. I first had to go by taxi and bus from Gaza to Cairo, then fly from Cairo to Amman. My wife and two kids, Yazzan, four, Yaffa, three (this was before we had our third child), were able to travel from Gaza to Amman through Israel. Of course, it was a tough journey for them, too. In Amman, we had to wait for fifty days for our visas. Then we traveled from Amman to Boston.

We were anxious and scared that the American officers at the airport would send us back, which had happened to a Palestinian student from Lebanon admitted to Harvard for his freshman year. They went through his social media and saw a few of his friends had posted things they considered "anti-American," and they turned him back. Even though Harvard intervened, he had to make the trip twice. Of course, if we were turned back, we would have no place to return to since our visit permits in Jordan had expired.

When our passports got stamped, tears filled my eyes, from relief I suppose.

The first thing I remember is traveling in a car on the highway at high speed and being aware that I was not seeing the rubble of destroyed buildings. Later, when we took some trips, I was astonished at the size of the country. Open lands, with trees and rivers. This world is big, it could be welcoming, accommodating, even comfortable. In Gaza, you imagine the world as a small place, and you never know what will hit you next, or from where.

It must have been very strange to have people eager to hear about you, your life, the Edward Said Library, and so on.

Everyone I met was eager to listen to me, to hear about my experience of living in Gaza, what life looks like there. In Gaza, I never received much appreciation for the libraries because of the political rifts, or because the people in charge haven't yet sensed how important the libraries are. The kind of support I felt in the U.S. meant a lot to me.

Of course, being so far away, and hearing about attacks in Gaza, made me worry about my family, to the point of not being able to sleep. I would message my brother and ask him to turn on the camera, just to see their faces, still alive.

After the year at Harvard, I got into the MFA Program at Syracuse and we moved there. But because of the pandemic, and classes being virtual, we felt very isolated and decided we should go back home to Gaza where I could finish the second semester online.

How do you think this experience of leaving Gaza and then going back has impacted you?

I think my experience of living and writing in the United States helped me to see myself in Gaza more clearly. Even when my body left Gaza, my soul was still there. In a poem that I wrote in Arabic while in the U.S., I asked the wind to take care of my shadows, the shadows I had left in the streets of Gaza. I asked the cars not to run over my shadow. My eyes had moved to the U.S., and looking at Gaza from afar, I could see the big picture. For example, "The Wound," the poem about my own experience of being wounded, is something I wrote in the U.S. I'm not sure if I could have written that in Gaza. I could see that experience as if it was being replayed. I was with the audience, and Gaza was on the screen. I could see the film. Mainly, it helped me to see myself, and my people, more clearly. Now when I'm in Gaza, I write almost like a reporter.

In the U.S., I could write about a tree bending down to drink from my teacup while I'm walking in the morning, or a squirrel sipping from a glass I left on the porch. But while I'm in Gaza, I can only think about the constant sound of the drones, the F-16s, the seashore littered with bodies or shrapnel.

All in all, my experience in the U.S. was very good. I was surprised how many people were aware of Palestine and Gaza, because I didn't think that would be the case. But being Palestinian, especially from Gaza, can also feel uneasy. When I needed to inquire as to whether I could return to Gaza through Egypt or Jordan, there was no embassy I could go to in the U.S. No matter where I am—in Gaza, in Palestine, if I could even get there, or in the United States—I remain stateless.

ABOUT THE AUTHOR

Mosab Abu Toha is a Palestinian poet, scholar, and librarian who was born in Gaza and has spent his life there. A graduate in English language teaching and literature, he taught English at the United Nations Relief and Works Agency (UNRWA) schools in Gaza from 2016 until 2019, and is the founder of the Edward Said Library, Gaza's first English-language library.

In 2019–2020, Abu Toha was a Visiting Poet in the Department of Comparative Literature at Harvard University; a Visiting Librarian at Harvard's Houghton Library; and a Religion, Conflict, and Peace Initiative Fellow in the Harvard Divinity School. In 2020, Abu Toha gave talks and readings at the University of Pennsylvania, Temple University, and the University of Arizona. He also spoke at the American Library Association (ALA) Midwinter Meeting held in Philadelphia in January 2020. In October 2021, Notre Dame's Literatures of Annihilation, Exile, & Resistance lecture series hosted Abu Toha to speak about his poetry and work in Gaza.

Abu Toha is a columnist for Arrowsmith Press, and his writings from Gaza have appeared in *The Nation*, Arrowsmith Press, and Literary Hub. His poems have been published on the Poetry Foundation's website, in *Poetry Magazine*, *Banipal*, *Solstice*, *The Markaz Review*, *The New Arab*, *Peripheries*, and other journals.

These poems have appeared previously in the following publications:

Leaving Childhood Behind, My Grandfather Was a Terrorist, A Voice from Beneath, Ibrahim Abu Lughod and Brother in Yaffa, Desert and Exile, To Mahmoud Darwish, To Ghassan Kanafani, Edward Said, Noam Chomsky, and Theodor Adorno: *Banipal*

my grandfather and home, Things You May Find Hidden in My Ear: *Poetry*

In the War: you and houses, My City After What Happened Some Time Ago, silence of water: *Peripheries*

Forever Homeless: *The Nation*

A Rose Shoulders Up: *The Markaz Review*